D1173791

Crocodiles

Leo Statts

abdopublishing.com

Published by Abdo Zoom™, PO Box 398166, Minneapolis, Minnesota 55439. Copyright © 2017 by Abdo Consulting Group, Inc. International copyrights reserved in all countries. No part of this book may be reproduced in any form without written permission from the publisher. Abdo Zoom™ is a trademark and logo of Abdo Consulting Group, Inc.

Printed in the United States of America, North Mankato, Minnesota
062016
092016

Cover Photo: Shutterstock Images
Interior Photos: Shutterstock Images, 1, 6, 7, 8–9, 16–17, 17; Marcus Lindstrom/iStockphoto, 5; iStockphoto, 10–11; Red Line Editorial, 11, 20 (left), 20 (right), 21 (left), 21 (right); Filipe Frazao/Shutterstock Images, 12; George Clerk/iStockphoto, 13; Stuart G. Porter/Shutterstock Images, 14; Andre Anita/Shutterstock Images, 15; Sergey Uryadnikov/Shutterstock Images, 18

Editor: Brienna Rossiter
Series Designer: Madeline Berger
Art Direction: Dorothy Toth

Publisher's Cataloging-in-Publication Data
Names: Statts, Leo, author.
Title: Crocodiles / by Leo Statts.
Description: Minneapolis, MN : Abdo Zoom, [2017] | Series: Swamp animals |
    Includes bibliographical references and index.
Identifiers: LCCN 2016941158 | ISBN 9781680792089 (lib. bdg.) |
    ISBN 9781680793765 (ebook) | ISBN 9781680794656 (Read-to-me ebook)
Subjects: LCSH: Crocodiles--Juvenile literature.
Classification: DDC 597.98--dc23
LC record available at http://lccn.loc.gov/2016941158

Table of Contents

Crocodiles

Crocodiles are big reptiles.
They look like alligators.
But they are not the same.
Crocodiles have pointier snouts.

Their snouts are shaped like a V.

Body

Crocodiles have tough skin.
Some are brown or black.

Others are green or tan.

A crocodile's eyes are on the top of its head.

So are its ears and nostrils.

Habitat

Crocodiles live in tropical places.
Many live in swamps.

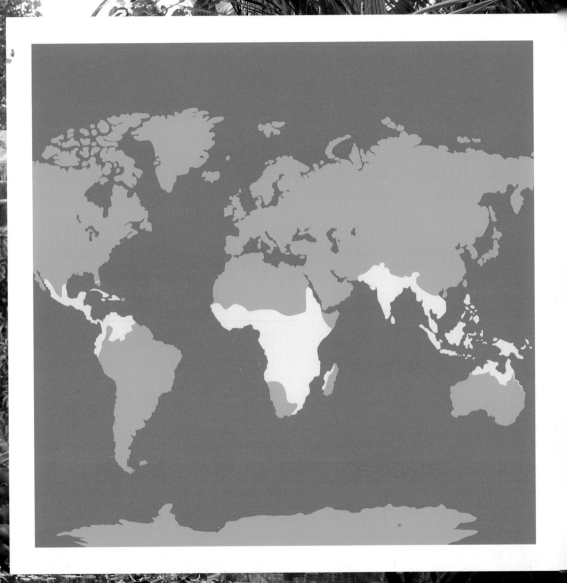

Where crocodiles live

Crocodiles spend lots of time in the water. They can swim fast.

Some can go
nine miles per hour (14.5 kmh).

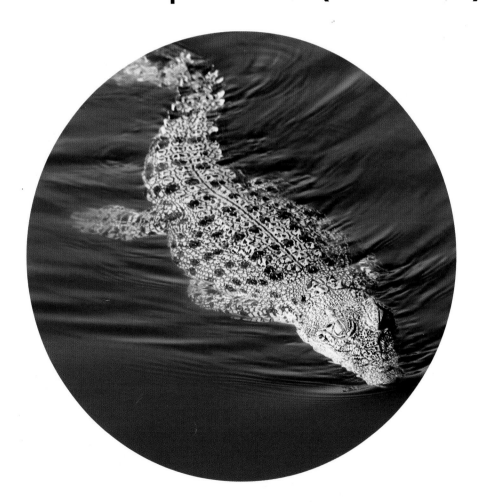

Crocodiles are **predators**.

They eat fish and birds. They also eat deer or zebras.

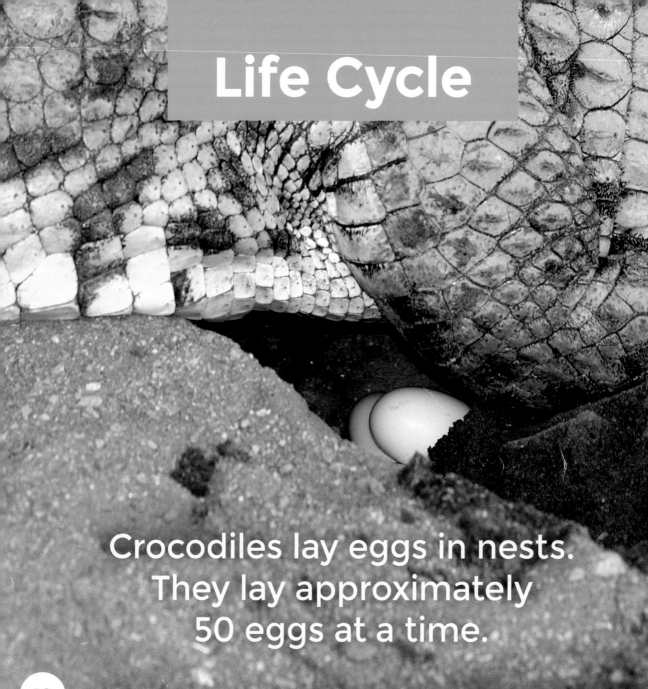

Life Cycle

Crocodiles lay eggs in nests.
They lay approximately
50 eggs at a time.

Babies **hatch** from the eggs.

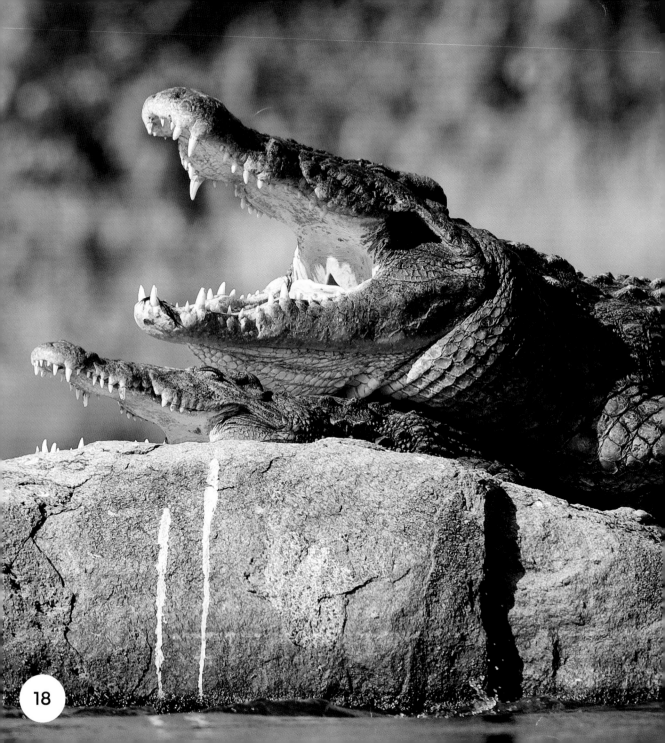

Crocodiles can live more than 60 years in the wild.

Quick Stats

Lightest Weight

A dwarf crocodile weighs more than a full suitcase.

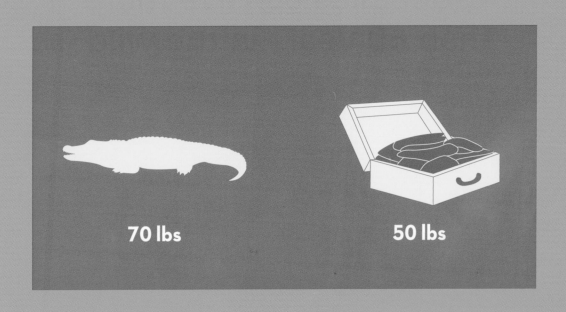

70 lbs

50 lbs

Heaviest Weight

A Nile crocodile is heavier than a soda vending machine.

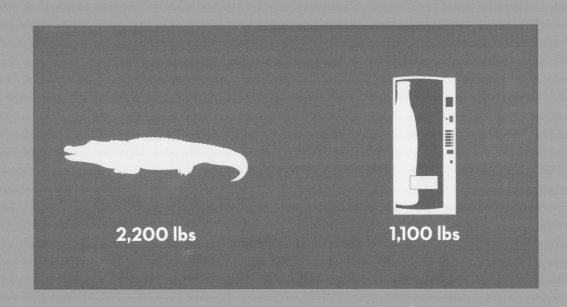

2,200 lbs   1,100 lbs

Glossary

hatch - to be born from an egg.

predator - an animal that hunts others.

reptile - a cold-blooded animal with scales. They typically lay eggs.

snout - a part of the face that sticks out. It has the nose and mouth.

swamp - wet land that is filled with trees, plants, or both.

tropical - weather that is warm and wet.

Booklinks

For more information
on crocodiles, please visit
booklinks.abdopublishing.com

Learn even more with the Abdo Zoom
Animals database. Check out
abdozoom.com for more information.

Index